Father Time

by Giles Ford

Sarn Athrad

Ford of Stones - Aubrey Ford 1925-2012

for Emma, Arthur and our next one..

Thank you Cyril, Provincetown, friends, fellowship, inspirers, writers and beyond

Father Butterfly

Today, a butterfly lay dying on the pavement
while shoppers bagged their way home, heads in the clouds
a good omen – you told me – a positive thing

you stopped and picked him up, gave him the back of your hand
criss-cross pattern of risen veins, to rest his wings
tightly shut together, not stirring, as if praying

you carried him held up, out in front of you
now and then sitting down, resting in the sun
then every few moments rising again and picking your way along the street

one foot in front of the other, watching
where each landed before the other took off again
light frame, slight tall body, awkward arms and legs

till finally you found a place to sit quietly, on a grey stone
to rest a moment longer, breathing still, holding your delicate visitor steady
on the mottled earth as you caught your breath together

before he opened his wings, sudden display, Persian carpet
and flew into the bush
a good omen – you told me – a positive thing

The Living and the Dead

I like to lie at the sea's edge, the spilling sea
and roll over and over the edge of the world
land, sky and sea, dot to dot eternity
stitched together by long shoreline thread
outlining the living and the dead

I like to lie at the sea's edge, the frothing sea
and let her turn and tumble me
the stinging sea – just her and me
variable palette of ferocity

Once I knew how to be ahead

I circle myself looking for clues
cues to speak, minor reflections

why are you with me?
I don't know who I am anymore

unformulated raw legs dangling
not mine, swing into the car

we hold hands, on each other's knees
brushing off the past

smiling at each other
we reach a plateau

I cannot open the bike lock today
I have lost my touch

the small things are defeating me
I cannot answer the telephone

which button to press?
Hello, Hello are you there?

why am I downstairs?
keys. Yes. Glasses. A different place every time

Please.

don't ask too many questions
I don't know where I am going

once I knew how to be ahead
now I wish for things even before my time

33's, 45's carbolic soap, 3 Television channels
and the farm horse drooping its mane over the broken fence

Stone

you have come a long way
don't know where from
how long you travelled
what route you took

I only know you came to me
glistening blue
in the Charmouth sun

I know you are one
amongst a million handfuls
jangled by the froth

chipped and chattered
in the seawave of stones
penduluming the beach

marking the passing time
washing in and out
oceanic metronome

Father Terradactil

I was peeling a banana and knew it was bad might be hiding a nasty bruise inside skin tore and split open ripe green threads dangling turned fat and faecal expanding in the air threw it in the sink where it began to twitch and writhe turn frothy gooey then breathe itself into a pulsating sac like blown bubble gum or throat of toad must kill it now before it grows too big smash and stamp upon its every living breathe but curious stood watching it burst forth flapping in the kitchen transparent blue sharp terradactil beak small eyes wings all points and angles turning its head this way and that veins risen fast snatched its trainagular bone lipped beak cold scissors in my fist firmly shut and carried it outside not knowing what to do felt a sudden sympathy for it and thought might let it fly not splinter and crush the baby underboot now all draining energy limp like bundle of old dish rags graying in my hands could not kill it then and took it back inside to tell me his story pleading quietly from his defeated body too late saw I had a dying angel in my hands

Father says

Father: I was thinking……my father was a farmer and my son is an artist

Son: an artist?

Father: Yes an artist. Yesterday, you walked into the sea, a turbulent sea and a wave took you and threw you around, tumbled you, scrunched you into the sand and out onto the beach – you were out of your depth.

But Cynthia was right. You are brave and it will get better and you'll learn.

Son: So what do you think makes me an artist Dad?

Father: You are happy (when you paint). It shows. There's an aura about you that comes from inside you, within you. It's not a job – it's from deep down.

Father Says

Yesterday was a good day.
It made me happy
Painting portraits of children
You going to Cynthia's'
Being an artist

Son Says

Why Art Dad?

Pause

Freedom son, Freedom

So you are not bound and trapped son, not imprisoned by society and systems.

Yes

Learn the tools and techniques son.

Learn the methods and materials

But then go beyond

And you will find yourself on your own

Original

Father Says:

Don't go looking too hard son
forcing yourself
thinking all the time
mind like a fretting flag
searching for the answer
there is more to life than wisdom

It's all been settled son
all you need is to
live your own life
and love the yellow butterfly
playing with pebbles
on the sand

Stone

every time I reach for you
you are there
you have much to tell me

I study you
quite
carefully

one one side
you are speckled
a galaxy in a grey night

on the other
speckled blue
like an egg

there is dark and light
within you
a groove on one edge

Father says:

Follow your own path son

Expect poverty and a degree of loneliness

But follow your self

Don't pay too much attention

To what others say or think

Everybody has their own different opinions

- Paint son, Write
- Go your own way
- Stick with it and keep going

Skimming Stones

Skimming stones you bend your body
dance low to the ground, in rehearsal,
taught arm, bowed, angled, el-bowed
movements like Degas, ballerina
wrist ready to turn, spin and hand flick
Father trick, you have the art
down to a T, body grooved
memory

you lose your balance
stone skims
only once
sinks
like a stone
I look away
pretend
not to see

then some skimpy success
– tiny little leaps
we are in a miniature world
life force measured out
in ripples

I laud and admire you. I praise you.
I describe the stones trajectory
how many times it skipped but
We both know I am lying

I pick a perfectly smooth stone and hold it
caress and soothe it.

I want to slip the stone in my pocket
to feel it now and then
but instead I take on the mantle

I take the stone in my hand and meld with it
I retract from the scrunching sand and the swaying boats
from the jangling boat bells calling, calling each other, calling us
and I dance as I was taught to dance

I hurl the stone, energy like teeth pouncing on the water over and over
cutting and running to the call of the distant herd then disappearing deep

I do not look behind me, or across
I wonder whether he was watching
I gloat and am afraid
I have won at last
in the moments before
everything I am about to lose
I am a betrayer
suddenly a man

'Beautiful son' he smiles

'Beautiful'.

Tired of being old

The door won't stay open
where it's meant to be
and the wind is misbehaving

Shit! The fucking phone.
who the hell is it now?
there's always something isn't there?

tinderbox of small resentments
powderkeg of old age, fuses long and short
waiting to be ignored

there are no cherry trees
laden with snow
in my garden

Stone

I will not let you go
I will hold you close
In the palm of my hand
I will treasure you

sometimes I am glad the world is blind
It allows me free reign
I do not have to hoard

I can leave you on the beaches turning into sand
I can leave you on the path kicked and scattered
I can skim you over the water and let them sink without a trace

except this one
In my pocket
In my hand

Son Says

Why aren't you wearing your hearing aides Dad?

Your hearing aides

Life would be a lot easier if you wore your hearing aides

Are they switched on?

Have the batteries run out?

Have you got your key?

And sweater? – for later on at least?

Did you eat Dad? What did you have for lunch?

Cereal?

Mind the step, the puddle, take it easy, slow down, take your cane.

Your cane.

No, No, it's not too slow for me.

I've got all the time in the world

Father Starling

Are the rooftops echoing

To the starlings flight

Darting

Diving

Swooping

Kniving

Are you still

Looking at the

Azelia tree

At the Wisteria

Clinging

Onto

Its age old story

are you walking in the cool corridor

of streets too deep for the Florentine sun

or have you gone home now

have you gone home?

Small boy with a stone

You reach out
to feel it's otherness
its secret gift

You reach out
spiritual
seeing things we don't

'Stone. Stone' you cry.

'Stone. Stone'.

Your heart is not

Home

I promised I would never do it
but perhaps there is no harm?
it might not be so bad
3 hot meals a day
and your own room
a book or two
a comfy chair?
to make you feel at home
we can visit every day
weekends
or maybe holidays?

The Gate

I know I am arguing with the gate
It is too tall for my liking, too thin and rickety
the paintwork is flecked and peeling
is scratched and ragged
there is green lichen growing in places
and I can see tiny holes bored
into some of the wood
It is the wrong colour
and does not fit its surroundings
the path way is uneven, broken, jagged
and clearly needs repairing
there are weeds at its feet
and one can no longer read the sign
it's a disgrace really
and I tell it so quite categorically
'You should be ashamed of yourself
How can you expect me to go through
such a gate - while you are in such a condition?
Not fully keeping up your end of the bargain'
I say.

I will not step through such a gate.

No. I will not.

Now you are the sand

I saw your broken body Dad
I stroked your face
and held your cold hand

Now you are the sea Dad
Now you are the sand
Now You are the sky Dad
and I feel your spirit
sweep across the land

I saw your broken body Dad
and I held your cold hand
Now you are the sea Dad
Now you are the sand.

Provincetown Bay / Low Tide Mist

White on white - lineless definition
mind drawing hull distinctions

In the beach mist a tall mast
fine straight charcoal line

The sea has inhaled exposing
mud flat palette, fluid draining, rivulets to source
reverse entropy beneath my feet

boats – a field of tethered horses, heads bowed
sleeping feetless, shouldering the early morning
sodden clam cockled graveyard

lobster pots, half drowned lanterns
chinese temples darken the rusting sand

a hermit crab tickles the air

I'm sorry

'I'm sorry' said the young black nurse

We were just talking round the corner...

I didn't know your father that well...so...

Another patient alerted us

Coroner

'I'm so sorry again about your mother Aubrey's death'
The Bath RUH coroner Alan said

'She died of natural causes' he said

'She?'

'Sorry. He'.

Not from his fall in the hospital?
Not from tripping over the wires and tubes climbing out of the intensive care bed desperate for some water?
Not from hitting his head on the oxygen bottle a few seconds before he died?

'No, not from that' he said. 'He had a number of conditions'.

Alan, the coroner, on his first call said it clearly shouldn't have happened
it was something that needed investigating properly
there really had to be a post mortem...it could be done in Bristol he said... but
he reassured me.... it was just as well kept in Bath

'Much easier' he said. 'Would save a journey back and forth'
And he knew the pathologist well.

'They won't brush anything under the carpet' he said
I wonder why he said that.

Looking you straight in the eye

I feel your hands
bony, delicate and gnarled
swift as a pickpocket

you are checking to see if I am ready
Go on. Take me. Take me
I am not afraid of you

totally surrendering to you
I become unpalatable
no-one desires the desirous

you flee into the night
to find a running soul
some-one who cannot bear to go

I release my succumbing
take back my body
disintegrate into sleep

merge with spirit
conscious unconsciousness
dismorphia

If I sleep
Will I wake?
will I recalibrate?

Stone

Out of my hand
you turn cold, thin
you lose your colour
you dim
I cannot see your stars

Photograph

sepia
delicate
small
found in a box
in the garage

its black and whiteness
older than my life
a time of
zig zag borders

saw you
as a soldier
as a young man
as a boy
Palestine 1947

placed you gently on my desk
on the mantelpiece
in an album to remember
I was loved once

the world is empty without you
too much space to be
the snow purifies the earth

Provincetown Bay

I have walked to the edge of the world
to place your ashes heavy with life
on some small bark washed ashore
this strand close to your heart

I have placed your ashes for the wind to soothe
to cusp and pirouette
carry you playful across the sand
mingle and merge

I wait loyal for the sea to come
and purify
while flying fish jump and rejoice
under the white disc of the sun

When they go

when they go
they go forever

no time to call from the airport
or send an inadequate postcard
saying you arrived safely

when they go
they go forever

saying only before they leave
'Don't drink to much will you son
Remember to take your coat, your hat, your scarf

I think there are still some sausage rolls in the fridge'.

Going swimming with my less than two year old son

'Swimmin, swimmin' you say 'Kick Kick'

You bring me my boots from the hall
dragging my worn out old black coat
pulling my hand towards the door handle

You know you are on your way

'Shoes on, Shoes on'
'Coat on, Coat on'

I scoop you up and leave the footed world behind
we become one creature dancing the waters
a ballet of timelessness

Driving Past

I drove to see you not there
down the long puddled lane
Past the nuzzling horses in the field
Past the skyline and tight hedgerows
Past the dipped pond and sheep hidden orchard
over the little humpbacked bridge by peeling church
to the crossroads where I used to turn right

Gas Fire

How can the world exist

without you in your green paisley chair?
by the gas fire glowing coals
watching cats and schoolchildren go to and fro

How can the world exist?

small teddy bears proliferate my dreams
and there is a light dusting of snow
blessing the earth

Stone

I search for you
In my pocket
you are not there

I need you to comfort me
to hold you in my hands
where are you?

I have left you
with my son
you are not lost

You have found
the place you
were first found

I see you

As I walk over to the green wooden Provincetown house
behind the mesh mosquito screen that clangs twice
magnifying glass in hand re-reading your diary
observing an object you have found
deciphering a letter you have been sent
or perhaps, pencil stub in hand, shading a portrait
you have been working on
or reading, holding your cold mug of tea
or maybe eating a late mid-afternoon bowl of cereal

I see you on my way back from the studio, the sea, the Wired Puppy, a meeting
to bring you a cup of coffee
to show you the latest painting
to see if you want to go for supper at Farlands
to tell you of my latest woes and indecisions
to sit in the low slung rackety 1950's wooden chair
to rise above the whole world for a moment
to hear your stories
to see how life drawing went
to while away the hottest part of the day
to ask how your book is going or
to potter about a bit and check the fridge for anything interesting
to watch you cutting up the old Kellogg's corn flakes boxes into strips
to absorb a little more of you and remember who I am

Stone

This stone
This blue stone
This small blue stone

I carry
    in my pocket
    in my hand

I search for it
amongst my keys
I mine for it

I know what I am seeking
what I am feeling for
its shape

its smoothness and edge
for the way life has cut it
moulded it

to fit in between my fingers
between my thumb roll
uneven and jagged

and soft too
there is plenty to hold onto
to turn over and over

I see you

wearing the t shirt I made for you
with the delicate pencil portrait of Marina on it
heading up Pearl street, easel in one hand, three legged stool in the other

wearing your hat with peaked visor
ripped jeans and brown shoes and now
your Cape Cod School of Art shirt

sitting in the shade of your favourite tree
on the bench with Peter O'Malley the balloon man
on the white wrought iron chair just inside the Egeli Gallery

in the distance down Commercial Street
In the crowd passing by Ellie still singing next to her sign
'76 years old and still a show girl!'

in Angel foods chatting
with your small bottle of water to last the day
outside Farlands bent double over the news

I see you on the beach smiling
walking the beach slower than gulls
sitting on the upturned blue boat in the sand

Bewilderment

the poet asked me
what's the story behind the story
what are you not writing about
what are you not saying
what are you resisting
turning away from

where are your thresholds

go deeper, deeper
into your bewilderment
to the place where the familiar
and the unknown touch each other

break down
be inarticulate

now that is really interesting

Poem

it doesn't take much to write a poem

just a thought, a feeling

a mayfly life

Silent Ovation

I cannot let go of those I have loved
they visit me in waking dreams
In the street
at night
in gestures
they hide behind you

surrounding me in ascendant circles
they visit in vain
amphitheatering
in silent ovation

they are tall and slender
polar spectres
blue white flame
in their ice
speechless pillars
stalactites telling me my story

some of them are still alive
unaware of their visitations

they paint and look after their twin daughters

they work in stone and bookshops
they wake up in the arms of their lovers and mothers
they become their father's father

Stone

I love this stone
this small stone
this small blue stone
I carry in my pocket

it holds the warmth
of your hand within it
the power of the sun
the wash of the waves

so much has been washed away
in your life:
a boulder, a clifftop
a mountain range

where did you come from stone?
who have you met?
what have you seen?
who else have you loved?

Leaving

Each time I gathered myself together
keys, glasses, hat. In that order?

you would smile fatherlove at me
as I set out to paint those snowdays

you would lean forward in your armchair and wave me good luck
through the moist, glittering innocent snow

You would smile fatherpride
as I buried myself deeper and deeper into my life

returning, you would wave at me again
your face lighting up the sun

and then you were gone.

No Seventh Heaven

I wear your ragged creased belt
that tightened like a corset
till there were no holes left to hold you together
and you had to puncture new ones

I shave with your old fashioned shaving brush
and double edged Wilkinson sword razor
circling your shaving cream in an old wooden bowl
preferring nicks and cuts to seven bladed heaven

Paisley chair

You are not in
your paisley chair
hunched over by the fire
with your magnifying glass
and your cold cup of tea resting
on the wobbly too small side table

you are not sifting through papers
trying to find the portrait you have lost
some where in the pile of books and postcards
and letters from old friends

You are not in the hallway
hands outstretched to single bannister
leading you up the stairs to the only bathroom
one step at a time, make sure you touch the edge

You are not tucking your duvet over
switching on the blow heater at five
closing the curtains to keep the cold out
or settling down for the evening news

You are not microwaving your hotpot

12 minutes only
Don't pierce the top, leave to stand for one minute
And eat with a slice of bread or two

You are not walking double caned
buttoned up tight against the wind
scarved and hatted, fingerless gloved
smiling up at your favourite tree

You are not

Strange House Strange House

Last night the wardrobe was restless
shifting itself from one foot to the other
clunking its doors to let me know
it was in some discomfort
the curtains shone see through
wearing their transparence
like a flimsy dress blowing in the wind
after the party is over

the carpet is complaining, has had enough
feels worn down and threadbare
shivering in the breeze
while the radiator pumps itself up
not willing to admit defeat
old trooper to the last

I lie awake and remember
long point and the sun diamonding the sea
our race across the dunes
and the seals loving us

Borgo degli Albizi 14

The Azelia tree still blooms
shedding its beauty

the shutters still hold out
the Florentine sun

the sky is still blue

the one legged club footed beggar
still plays the street like a heron beside the waters

the café bartender still serves gruff
chequered behind his marble table top

the children still play in Plaza D'Azelia looking out for the old man
on the bench drawing pencil portraits

Today

I know there is something missing
what did I not do?
what did I not say?

I think and did all the things a son should do:

- wait for you to come home from work at 6 playing with Lego by the front door
- jump up and hug you in your snow driven fur coat
- make you flinch with my fearlessness on the metal playground
- skate with you on the townhall ice rink and swim the whole lake
- take your side no matter what mum said
- try and hit your bowling for six every time
- play rugby ferociously
- not write home
- drink too much
- ask for money
- lose my way
- blame you for everything
- learn the hard way
- fight Death for you

Poem

Don’t try to hard
to say something
important or beautiful son

we all know poems
are just words
nothing less

marks we make
to reassure ourselves
we can still love

3 cups of tea

I sift and filter
memories
cloudy, stony, swirling
until the day intervenes

Orphan

I remember too much and not enough
to comfort me as I see your body lying
where they laid you out cold

I reach out my hand to fit in yours
the only place it ever felt safe
in the world you held up for me

My Son's Stars

he had a handful of them
on his fingertips
and gave them to me
to carry in my pocket
to take with me everywhere
and place in the sky
when I needed find my way home

I sift and filter through your life

Object by Object
Old Newspaper by Old Newspaper
Letter by Letter
Postcard by Postcard
Trinket by Trinket
Box by Box
Memory by Memory
Photogaph by Photograph
Old love by old love
Loss by loss
Diary by Diary
Day by Day
Entry by entry
Poster roll by Poster roll
Button by button
Medal by Medal
Book by Book
Underline by Underline
Highlight by highlight
Tear by Tear

One Year on

And you are still gone

I hoped I might find you again
sitting in the armchair by the window
by Pilgrims monument overlooking the bay
in the far end bedroom
swinging your long john legs from beneath the covers
shuffling to and from the bathroom reaching out with fingertips
                    chair
                    wadrobe
                    either side of door frame
on your way to a cup of tea

I thought I might see you
on the town hall bench with your sign
                    Free children's portraits
                    When: now
                    How long: 2 hours
                    Where: Here

I thought I might catch a glimpse of you
making your way down Commercial Street
or by the bookstore window
bent over not quite double reading the outdoor newsrack
Or cycled by on pedicab waving and smiling with joy.

Moon

tonight
a full moon in a dark sky
ultra marine
so blue it could be black

I know you are there

I sit opposite you
never in your chair
I wave as I leave the house
I wave as I bicycle past the bay
on my way to paint and on my way back
I peer in to see you past the window reflection
to catch a glimpse of your white hair
to see you smiling fatherlove
to marvel at your translucence

I remember you waving me off awaiting my return
I remember bringing you back trophies
photographs of the days brushstrokes
tales of etching, layering, scraffiti
and we would sift through the days
and dream of what memories we would create next

More than 15 minutes grieving is self-pity

Lewie said to me over pancakes thick with
STOP & SHOP own brand no maple syrup
as we honoured your life

'What a man! What a man!

He knew how to live
that enough is a feast
to eat to live not live to eat
that less is more
to live with grace
and leave no tracks
to shake your cane in the street when needed

He touched a thousand lives
drawing portraits of children in the street
and giving them away free

Who else would do that today -
Tell me?
Who else?

Lewie's Poem

When he first came here
the town was totally alive, totally alive - you could see it moving and swaying
and the air was full of the smell of fish and paint, fish and paint
and everyone was a character in those days - each and every one stood out
and the town was totally alive- moving and swaying
and there were easels and artists up and down the street
all the way to the pier and the sea
and the air was alive with the smell of fish of fish, of fish and paint

England

now I know why you sought solace

in the robin and the snow laden branch

the child's mittened wave

and the glitter of the diamond sea

Sometimes

I catch myself thinking
must remember to tell Dad about that

Why Wait?

I look forward to being a crazy old man
with a big beard and pink sneakers
I will make Gustav Klimt look dapper, wear Edwardian tufts
and grow eyebrows like an Owls

I will wake up late and read poetry to the postman
eat Chunky Monkey for breakfast, swim with seals
and stop only to talk to flowers

I will walk the dunes for days searching
for the end of the shoreline
and chase places not even rainbows have found

I will drift through life without a trace
like the gentle Provincetown breeze
wearing ripped jeans and paint splatters

I will sculpt children's stories, drink tea with Mary Oliver
and gaze out all day till I too become the waves
found where the sky and the land meet the sea

Who are you? A Poem by Aubrey Ford

Who are you?
lying on the forest floor
watching the stars
dancing through the leaves?

Who are you?

I am the pearl in the oyster
waiting to be discovered
beneath the ocean wave
on the ocean floor.

Who are you?

Giles Ford is a poet, writer and secret Chunkey Monkey eating painter who lives in Somerset & Provincetown (whenever he can), with his beautiful love Emma, his star fingered son Arthur, one darling to come and their old sneezing cat, Bifty.
To find out more about Giles' writing visit 'Giles Ford Writers' on facebook and to if you'd like to see Giles's paintings visit www.gilesfordart.com *and* www.kobaltgallery.com

www.ingramcontent.com/pod-product-compliance
Ingram Content Group UK Ltd.
Pitfield, Milton Keynes, MK11 3LW, UK
UKHW020233250726
13967UKWH00001B/343